The Ghosts of Scotland: A Collection of Ghos
Nation

By Sean McLachlan and Charles River Editors

Anne Burgess' picture of a Pictish Stone

About Charles River Editors

Charles River Editors provides superior editing and original writing services across the digital publishing industry, with the expertise to create digital content for publishers across a vast range of subject matter. In addition to providing original digital content for third party publishers, we also republish civilization's greatest literary works, bringing them to new generations of readers via ebooks.

Sign up here to receive updates about free books as we publish them, and visit Our Kindle Author Page to browse today's free promotions and our most recently published Kindle titles.

About the Author

Sean McLachlan spent many years working as an archaeologist in Europe, the Middle East, and the United States. Now a full-time writer, he's the author of many history books and novels, including *A Fine Likeness*, a Civil War novel with a touch of the paranormal. Feel free to visit him on his Amazon page and blog.

Introduction

Finlay McWalter's picture of the William Wallace Monument

Weird Scotland

"In Scotland, beautiful as it is, it was always raining. Even when it wasn't raining, it was about to rain, or had just rained. It's a very angry sky." – Colin Hay

Scotland is a fascinating and ancient land filled with history. It has produced explorers, warriors, inventors, writers, and more than a few murderers. For many centuries, it fought bitter wars against England to maintain its independence, and even when those wars were finally lost, Scotland retained its distinct culture and identity. Though a part of the United Kingdom, it would be a mistake to lump it in with England, Wales, and Northern Ireland, as Scotland has its own tales to tell and traditions to maintain.

Not everything in Scotland is as it appears, however. Some Scots say this is a land haunted by spirits, a place of strange disappearances and unexplained phenomena. There is no shortage when it comes to the strange stories Scotland has to offer, and the legends and lore have compelled many to dig a little deeper and even explore this wonderful land for themselves.

Some of those tales are downright grisly. Scotland has always been a rival to its southern neighbor, and the rivalry extends to the number of hauntings in its medieval castles, stately homes, and old cobblestone streets. While many Englishmen claim that their country is the most haunted, the Scots can point to their own stories of ghosts as evidence they may beat the English in this dubious distinction.

The Ghosts of Scotland: A Collection of Ghost Stories across the Scottish Nation is a collection of such tales, just a few among the thousands of local legends and modern sightings that make Scotland one of the most haunted countries in the world. It is part of a collection of other books written by Sean McLachlan, including *The Ghosts of England: A Collection of Ghost Stories across the English Nation* and *The Ghosts of Ireland: A Collection of Ghost Stories across the Emerald Isle*. For other strange occurrences in Scotland, ranging from Nessie to jelly falling from the sky, check out another title in the series, *Weird Scotland: Monsters, Mysteries, and Magic Across the Scottish Nation*. Along with pictures of important people, places, and events, you will learn about the ghosts of Scotland like never before.

The Ghosts of Scotland: A Collection of Ghost Stories across the Scottish Nation
About Charles River Editors
About the Author
Introduction
   Haunted Castles
   Haunted Roads
   Edinburgh
   Haunted Pubs and Churches
   Remote Ghosts
   Online Resources
   Bibliography
Free Books by Charles River Editors
Discounted Books by Charles River Editors

Haunted Castles

Scotland's past was a violent one, from bitter struggles between Highland clans to invasions from England and Scandinavia, resulting in a landscape filled with castles. From small family forts to massive military establishments and royal domains, Scotland is estimated to have some 3,000 castles. Many of these have witnessed violent sieges, political prisoners walled up in dungeons and allowed to starve to death, and bloody family feuds. Is it any wonder that so many of Scotland's castles have a reputation for being haunted?

One castle with a long history of hauntings is Bedlay Castle, a few miles outside of Glasgow. Built in the late 16th century as a tower house - a fortified stone tower with living facilities - a succession of owners have expanded it over the years to make it larger and more comfortable for those who had to live there. Larger it certainly became, but not more comfortable, as generation after generation of residents have been terrorized by ghosts, such as that of a large bearded man said to be Bishop John Cameron (in office 1426-1446), one of the Bishops of Glasgow. His life ended well before the tower house was built, but there had been a residence for bishops on the site that has long since disappeared. Bishop Cameron has lingered, however, probably because his soul can't find rest. The bishop was found face down in a nearby loch, and many at the time believed he was murdered. If this is true, the killers got away, but legend has it he has wandered the area for centuries and is often seen walking into rooms in the house, perhaps in search of those who cut his life short. He is one of Scotland's most enduring ghosts.

There is also a phantom coach that travels down a nearby road between Glasgow and Sterling. It was an old coaching road in the days when horse-drawn coaches were the only form of public transport. Phantom coaches such as this are a mainstay of ghost sightings across the British Isles. In this case, the coach stops in front of the startled eyewitness, and a young girl in historic costume steps out. As soon as her foot touches the ground, the air splits with a loud scream, and the girl and the coach both disappear.

Not all the manifestations are visible. Residents in the castle have complained of hearing footsteps down empty corridors and feeling invisible fingers touch their hair.

In his 1856 book *Rambles Around Glasgow*, folklorist Hugh MacDonald discusses the ghost of the bearded man in skeptical detail:

> "Bedlay House has, or at least had, the unenviable reputation of being haunted. Who or what the ghost was while in the flesh we have been unable to discover, but that something uncannie [sic] had been seen or heard about the place is, or we should perhaps say was, very generally believed over the neighbourhood [sic]. One old man informed us seriously that it was a bad laird of former days who could not get rest in his grave. 'He was a sair trouble to a' about him (quoth our informant) when he was leevin', and I think it's rather too bad that he should get leave to come

back and disturb decent folk after he's dead.'

"According to fireside gossip[,] a party of ministers were on one occasion called in to lay the unquiet spirit; and we are assured, on the authority of an old man whose father held the reverend gentlemen's horses while they were engaged in the work, that when they came out of the house afterwards, 'the very sweat was pouring down their faces.' Whether the holy men succeeded in giving the ghost its quietus, or whether the general spread of knowledge, as is perhaps more likely, has put it to flight, we do not know, but one thing is certain, and that is, that there is now considerable doubts among the people of Chryston with regard to its existence. One gudewife, whom we question on the subject while she is filling her pitcher at Bedlay well, says, 'It's my honest opinion there was mair clash than onything else in the ghost story; and for my part I dinna believe ae word o't.'"

Later residents in the castle beg to differ because the hauntings continued throughout the 20th century.

Another haunted castle is one of Scotland's oldest. Duntrune Castle by Loch Crinan in Argyll was built in the 12th century and has the distinction of being the oldest continually inhabited castle in mainland Scotland. Standing atop a small peak overlooking the loch, it makes for an impressive sight, and for a long time, it served as one of a chain of castles built by the MacDougall clan to protect their territory, but it was later taken by the powerful Clan Campbell. This clan was constantly trying to expand its lands and made many enemies, including the Clan MacDonald. In 1644, the MacDonalds besieged the castle, and it was around this time that the castle apparently acquired its ghost.

Patrick Mackie's picture of the ruins of the castle

Macdonnel Coll Ciotach of Ulster marched with a large host through Campbell lands destroying everything in his path. Hearing that the Campbells had a stout fortress at Loch Crinan, he sent his piper to scout the castle, look for weaknesses, and report back to him. The piper pretended to be a wandering musician and asked for entry to the castle. The Campbells became instantly suspicious of his motives for visiting during wartime but admitted him—leading him straight to a cell in one of the towers. Oddly, they let him keep his pipes.

The piper had seen enough of the castle to know that his master would have no chance of taking it, so he peered out the window day and night, waiting to see Macdonnel Coll Ciotach's ships come up the loch as they had planned.

At last, the ships appeared, and the piper began to play the pibroch "The Piper's Warning to his Master." When Macdonnel Coll Ciotach heard the tune, he knew the piper was telling him to retreat, and he turned his ships around.

Of course, the Campbells had heard the pipe music, too. Realizing what the piper had done, they cut off all of his fingers so he could never play again. The piper bled to death, but ever since, the faint notes of "The Piper's Warning to his Master" can occasionally be heard through the stone corridors of the castle, sending chills up the spine of anyone who hears them.

Much later, the story had a startling confirmation when workers renovating the old castle came across a grave containing a skeleton missing both its hands, which had been cleanly cut off at the wrists, and buried according to Episcopalian rites. Many clans at the time, the MacDonalds included, were Episcopalian, but the Campbells were Presbyterian. The handless body was reinterred, but this did not stop the hauntings, and the piper continues to play his ghostly tune. In 1792, the castle and its ghostly piper were sold to Clan Malcolm, and it continues to serve as the clan seat to this day.

What hasn't changed much is the old clan territory around Loch Fyne, Argyll, on Scotland's west coast, which remains an area of natural beauty, with lonely shorelines, large areas left for animal grazing, and several little villages dotting the landscape. This has been traditional MacLachlan land for centuries, the clan stubbornly defending it against rival clans and the English. The MacLachlans also took part in many uprisings against the English as loyal Jacobites.

In 1745, rumors spread that Charles Edward Stuart had returned from exile to raise an army to fight for the Jacobite cause, which was nothing short of putting the House of Stuart back on the British throne. Everyone in Scotland—from the most powerful clan chiefs to the humblest shepherd—had to think long and hard about which side to take. The English had a much more powerful army than the clans, but for some, loyalty to the Jacobite cause was even more powerful.

Bonnie Prince Charlie

Lachlan MacLachlan, 17th chief of the Clan MacLachlan, sought the advice of Master Harry, the brownie that lived in the cellars of the castle. He was a tricky spirit, always playing pranks and scaring people, but he was also a staunch supporter of Clan MacLachlan, and in this grave hour, the clan chief knew he could trust the brownie's opinion. He found Master Harry beside himself with worry, saying that a stranger was coming from the north who would lead Lachlan to his death.

The clan chief knew the stranger must be the Bonnie Prince Charlie, Charles Edward Stuart.

Though he was worried about the brownie's words, Lachlan could not abandon the man whom he saw as the rightful king. He rallied his men and got ready to join him, but when he mounted his horse, the animal grew skittish and turned three times counterclockwise, a bad omen.

The brownie and the horse had seen the future. At the Battle of Culloden on April 16, 1746, Lachlan MacLachlan was killed by an English cannonball. Many other men of the clan fell as well. There is a mass grave on the battlefield of Culloden, with a headstone bearing the MacLachlan name. Clan lore says that Lachlan's horse galloped back to Castle Lachlan on the shore of Loch Fyne. When the residents saw the riderless horse, they knew their clan chief was dead.

Built in the 15th century, Castle Lachlan is of unusual design, with a rectangular layout, two residences, and a central courtyard within. After the English had won the battle, they set about destroying the strongholds of any clan opposing them, and old Castle Lachlan was no exception. The English sent a warship up Loch Fyne and bombarded the castle until it was a ruin. It was never rebuilt but remains an atmospheric ruin at the edge of the loch. Everyone left. Some of them were hunted by the authorities while others managed to escape. The only resident remaining at the castle was the Lachlan MacLachlan's loyal steed, which refused to leave until the day it died.

Some of the ruins of Castle Lachlan

According to lore, the horse is still there. Sometimes at night, the ruined walls of the castle echo with the sound of its whinnying and its hooves striking stone. Some hikers have even glimpsed it galloping to the castle, its saddle still empty.

Indeed, it doesn't take long to find allegedly haunted castles in Scotland, as the hauntings start just as visitors get to the border between England and Scotland. Berwick-upon-Tweed is located just over two miles south of the current border in the English county of Northumberland, and it has been fought over by the English and Scots for centuries. For much of its history, Berwick-upon-Tween was a Scottish town, and many believe it is still home to a very Scottish ghost.

Berwick Castle, which dates back to Norman times and was the scene of much of the fighting, now stands in ruins, but at least one old occupant allegedly still resides there. On moonlit nights, some people have seen a Highland bagpiper in full regalia, standing atop the crumbled battlements, playing a ghostly tune. He is most often seen standing close to a steep flight of stone steps, locally referred to as "the breakneck stairs." Is the piper commemorating the accidental death of some long-departed Scot--perhaps himself?

An 18th century depiction of Berwick Castle

The ruins of the castle today

Haunted Roads

The piper isn't the only ghost in Berwick-upon-Tweed. All three bridges spanning the River Tweed have their own ghosts. The oldest bridge, named Berwick Bridge, or by the local and not particularly original name of Old Bridge, was built in the early 17th century. At times the gray, blurry figure of a hooded monk can be seen walking across this historic span.

The Royal Border Bridge is a railway bridge built by famous railway engineer Robert Stephenson in 1850 at the dawn of the railway era. He was the son of George Stephenson, who built the world's first inter-city railway line between Liverpool and Manchester, in 1830. Robert Stephenson followed in the footsteps of his father and helped the railroad crisscross England. The Royal Border Bridge is one of his masterpieces, being 2,162 ft (659 m) long, with 28 arches rising 121 ft (37 m) above the river. Robert died in 1859, and has often been seen since, stalking the railway bridge at night, still admiring his creation.

Robert Stephenson

A third bridge, opened in 1928, is haunted by the ghost of a worker who died during its construction. It is one of the many constructions worldwide that are home to spirits of the men who died while building them.

In Scotland proper, the ghosts seemingly only get thicker. On the border, they tend to stick to travel routes and old buildings, and there are even entire stretches of roads that are considered haunted. The most notorious is the A75, especially the Kinmount Straight section in southwest Scotland, locally known as the "Ghost Road." This stretch of highway has seen numerous paranormal encounters for more than half a century.

The earliest sighting dates to 1957, when a truck driver passing along the A75 at night saw a couple walking, arm in arm, right across the road in front of him. He slammed on his brakes and was convinced he'd hit them. Once he'd pulled over, he jumped out of his vehicle to search for the bodies, but the couple had vanished.

A more dramatic apparition happened in 1962, when Derek and Norman Ferguson were driving along the road at around midnight. Suddenly, a large hen flapped up towards their windshield. The two men were startled, but not spooked. Anyone who has spent time driving in rural areas has had at least one near miss, thanks to a stray farm animal. Chasing after the hen came an old woman, waving her arms at the car. At first, the two men thought this was the owner of the animal, but then their experience got weirder. Right behind the old woman came a screaming man with long hair, followed closely by a menagerie of wild dogs, giant cats, hens, goats, and some creatures the Fergusons couldn't identify.

They didn't have long to look, as all of the people and the creatures disappeared in an instant. By this time, they had stopped the car. Suddenly, they felt the temperature plunge, and the car began to rock violently from side to side as if by an unseen force. Derek, either bravely or foolishly, got out of the car and the movement stopped as abruptly as it had started. He got back in, shaken and bewildered, only to see a large van come barreling down the street at them. It vanished just before hitting them.

The detail about the temperature going down is an interesting one. Paranormal investigators believe that ghosts draw ambient energy from the air around them, which causes the temperature to plunge. The more energy they require, the more the temperature will go down. The Fergusons felt the temperature go down quickly, just before the unseen spirits rocked their car. Some specialists in the spirits of the dead theorize that a ghost's need for energy is one of the reasons they are so rarely seen during the daytime. The power of the sun overwhelms them, it being too powerful for them to manifest in their weakened state, and thus blanks them out.

It's interesting that the ghosts that came at the Fergusons seemed to be trying to communicate with the land of the living. Garson and Monica Miller were driving at around 60 mph along the road one night in March of 1995, when suddenly a man stepped out, right in front of them. He looked to be middle aged, but rather strange. He had an empty sack folded on top of his head, and held what appeared to be a rag in his hands as he outstretched his arms towards the car. They didn't get much of a look, because they were going too fast. Like other drivers on this stretch of road, they were convinced they had hit what they'd thought was a regular human being, but when they screeched to a halt and went back to look, there was, of course, no trace of him. The couple was so concerned, they filed a police report.

The police received another baffling report in July of 1997, when Donna Maxwell was driving along the A75 with her two children. As with the other apparitions, a man stepped out into the road, right in front of her. Maxwell described him as being in his 30s with short hair, a red top, and dark pants. He, too, disappeared upon impact. She filed a police report, and apparently was so convincing, that the police didn't dismiss her story, but rather, issued a description of the man, asking the public for any clues. No one had seen the incident or reported a man with that description who had been injured in a car accident.

In another encounter back in 2012, a long-distance truck driver had parked on the Kinmount Straight portion of the A75, and took a nap in the back of his truck. The fellow must not have been a local, because no one familiar with the area would have ever considered doing that! He woke up at three in the morning with a dreadful sense of foreboding. When he looked out the window, he saw a long column of bedraggled people in what appeared to be medieval peasants' rags. Some were pushing handcarts as they trudged down the road like refugees. Others have seen this grim cavalcade, too.

The medieval refugees seem to be the only repeat performers on the A75. While hauntings in most places are typified by the same ghost appearing again and again, like the ghostly piper of Berwick Castle, the A75 ghosts are unusual for their variety, including everything from hens to eyeless phantoms.

The hauntings on the A75 Kinmount Straight fall into a pattern seen on many haunted roadways in the British Isles. Phantom travelers who suddenly disappear have been a part of road lore, probably as long as there have been roads, but with the invention of the automobile, they took on a different flavor. Now, instead of a farmer meeting a ghostly apparition at night while walking home from the May Fair or harvesting, a motorist will catch a glimpse of a ghost and think they have run it over. When they go to investigate, the ghost has disappeared. The A75 Kinmount Straight is not the only haunted road in Scotland, but it is the quintessential one.

Edinburgh

If the A75 is the most haunted road in Scotland, Edinburgh must be the most haunted city. This ancient center of Scottish life has been witness to some of the great events of Scottish history, and at the same time, has been a place of misery for many common people. Much of the central part of the city is a UNESCO World Heritage Site. Dominating the skyline is the great rocky hill atop which looms Edinburgh Castle, recently voted the top UK Heritage Attraction in the British Travel Awards. First built in the 12th century, it has been added to over the generations and is now an impressive site to visit for its fine views of the city, its several museums, and its storied past.

The city's most conspicuous landmark is Edinburgh Castle, sitting high atop a rocky eminence that dominates the surrounding countryside. It is a truly magnificent sight, having served as a defensive position since Celtic times, from at least the 2nd century AD. It started off being a fortress for the kings of Scotland, as early as the reign of King David I (1124-1153). Like many Scottish castles, it was the scene of bitter fighting on numerous occasions, having been besieged at least 26 times in its history, and perhaps more, since its early history is poorly known. Now it hosts numerous public events, and is a fascinating historic site where visitors get to see various museum displays, the Crown Jewels of Scotland, and the enormous medieval cannon, Mons Meg.

Kim Traynor's picture of Edinburgh Castle

Much of the paranormal activity in the castle comes in the form of strange sounds. Phantom drummers can be heard at night, calling the men to defend the battlements, and the castle wardens report strange knockings in locked and supposedly empty buildings. There is also a spectral piper who is heard but not seen, and a drummer who almost nobody wants to see because he's missing his head! The spirits manifest in other ways, too, such as sudden drops in temperature. Some people have also said they've felt an invisible hand tugging on their clothing, or touching their face.

At the foot of the castle is the Old Town, dating back to the early Middle Ages. Now clean and visitor-friendly, it was once a hellhole of overcrowded tenements, filthy streets, narrow lanes clogged with trash, and the occasional dead body. Space was at a premium, so most roads were narrow, and the buildings were some of the tallest of their age, rising six or more stories, leaving the narrow paths in almost perpetual darkness. Beneath this tangle of buildings is a warren of tunnels that attracted the poorest of the poor who went there in search of shelter, often dying unnoticed in the dark.

Beyond the Old Town is the newer and more orderly New Town, started in the 18th century to relieve overcrowding. An early example of urban planning, its Georgian and neoclassical architecture make for a pleasant contrast with the Old Town's more somber buildings.

Edinburgh has been home to many famous people who have left their mark on the fields of science and the arts, Alexander Graham Bell, pioneer of the telephone, was born there, as was John Napier, the mathematician who invented logarithms. Sir Arthur Conan Doyle, the creator of Sherlock Holmes, was born in New Town, and *Treasure Island* author Robert Lewis Stevenson lived there, as well. The city was also home to a fair number of murderers, thieves, and conmen, attracted by the excitement of living in a big city and its easy access to wealthy victims.

One of its more sinister residents was Major Thomas Weir. At first glance, he seemed the very model of an upstanding citizen. Born in 1599, he had a long military career before settling down in Edinburgh in his later years and becoming captain of the Town Guard. He was known throughout the town as a strict Presbyterian who never missed a church meeting, kept a chaste life, and lived with his sister, Jean (often referred to in sources as "Grizel").

They made their home on the West Bow, a curving street leading from the Royal Mile's wealthy homes and shops down to the lower town filled with slums and cheap drinking dens. Bow Street was a bastion against the low-lives from the lower town, held as such by well-to-do Presbyterians such as Major Weir, dubbed the "Bowhead Saints."

A depiction of Major Weir's house

Major Weir was a familiar sight about town with his military bearing, stern visage, and the black, Thornwood staff—carved with satyrs' heads—he always carried. These lusty pagan creatures from classical mythology were an odd choice for such a man to have on his staff, but no one thought much of it or the fact that he never failed to carry it.

One Sunday in 1670, Weir stood up to address the congregation, clutching his trusty staff as he always did, but instead of giving the usual sermon on sin and God's wrath, he shocked his fellow churchgoers with a lengthy, lurid confession of how he was a warlock. He recounted, in vivid detail, how he had been having an incestuous relationship with his sister for years. In addition, he had enjoyed carnal relations with various women and even some animals. The assembly sat and stared for a while, not believing their ears. Finally, they rose up and grabbed him. They would never have believed they had a warlock in their midst unless Major Weir had himself admitted to being one.

The law was initially reluctant to charge a pillar of the community with such foul crimes and suggested the man had either gone insane or was senile. He was 70 years old, after all, quite an advanced age for the time, but when they questioned his sister, Jean, she backed up the tales, embellishing them with her own details of having met with the Devil and riding around the countryside in a fiery coach. She also claimed that Major Weir's black Thornwood staff with the satyrs' heads had been a present from the Devil himself and was the key to his power.

In the face of such confessions, the court had no choice but to convict. The siblings were sentenced to execution by strangulation, which meant they were to be strapped to chairs atop a platform in front of a cheering crowd, with ropes looped through holes in the backs of the chairs that were tightened with a handle, slowly crushing the necks of the condemned. It was traditional for the executioner to tell the people to repeat the line, "Lord be merciful to me," so it would be their last statement before having the life choked out of them. Instead, Major Weir stated, "Let me alone. I will not. I have lived as a beast, and I must die as a beast." The execution proceeded, and afterward, his body was thrown into a fire to purify it. The executioner threw Weir's famous staff in after him, and many witnesses swore they saw it writhe like a snake and refuse to catch fire for many long minutes before it finally expired.

Jean went out in a similarly dramatic fashion. As they brought her up to the scaffold and the strangulation chair, she tore off her clothes and exposed herself to the assembled onlookers.

After their deaths, no one wanted to live in the Weirs' nice home on West Bow. It had been cursed, people whispered, and the spirits of the evil siblings still lingered there. For a hundred years before its final demolition, the property remained vacant, though the district was popular, save the activity there on some nights when lights are seen in the windows and baleful laughter resonates from within. Some have even heard the whirl of Jean's spinning wheel. What she could be spinning after death is anyone's guess. Sometimes, Major Weir makes an appearance on the street, galloping away on a headless black horse, no doubt on a mission to take care of the Devil's foul business.

The famous author, Robert Louis Stevenson, who was born and raised in Edinburgh, remembered growing up hearing tales of the strange transformation of these two pillars of Christian society. Literary critics believe this story to be the inspiration for his famous novel, *Dr. Jekyll and Mr. Hyde*.

Some sources say that Major Weir and his sister were the last people to be executed for witchcraft in Scotland, but this is incorrect. That dubious distinction goes to Janet Horne, who was burned at the stake for being a witch in 1727. She was also accused of riding her daughter to visit the Devil and having the girl shod like a horse. The older woman showed signs of senility, and the daughter had deformed hands and feet, sparking the imagination of superstitious neighbors who spread all sorts of accusations about the pair, claiming all of their troubles were the result of their practicing witchcraft.

Janet was stripped naked, smeared with hot tar, and paraded through the town of Dornoch in a barrel. Then she was taken to the spot where she was to be burned at the stake. The woman is said to have smiled at the crowd as she warmed herself by the fire that would soon kill her. Her daughter was also found guilty but managed to escape.

Scotland got rid of the death penalty for witchcraft nine years later, but there have been several extrajudicial killings since that time. If one walks downhill on West Bow and takes a left on Grassmarket, he or she will come to Greyfriars Kirkyard, the site of one of Scotland's most notorious poltergeists. A poltergeist is a particular kind of entity. Some say it's a ghost, while others claim it to be a different creature altogether. Poltergeists do not visually appear, but rather, make themselves known by moving or throwing objects and making sounds, like rapping on walls and furniture. The word comes from the German for "noisy spirit."

One spirit in the graveyard is noisier than any other poltergeist ever recorded. It is the shade of Sir George Mackenzie, often referred to as "Bloody Mackenzie." Born in Dundee sometime in the 1630s, Mackenzie rose to prominence in the legal profession and served as Justice-Depute between 1661 and 1663. During this time, he presided over several witch trials, and what is perhaps unusual for this era, he dismissed the charges, claiming the witches had suffered from mental illness, senility, or that they had been the victims of scurrilous rumors started by their neighbors. Modern historians agree, but it was a daring stance to take at the time. He also became a member of the Scottish Parliament for the County of Ross. In 1677, he was appointed Lord Advocate of Scotland, the highest legal position in the land, at which point, his reputation for tolerance and open-mindedness seems to have fled him.

Mackenzie

At that time, Scotland was being ripped apart by a religious struggle. A traditionalist Presbyterian movement, called the Covenanters, resisted English attempts at installing a new liturgy and eventually, Episcopalianism in Scotland. The fight had been going on for several decades, and it was Mackenzie's job to put a stop to it, solidifying England's rule over Scotland. One of the key tenets in Episcopalianism is that the monarch is the head of the Church, something to which most Presbyterians object since it smacks of Catholicism.

In 1679, matters came to a head when the Covenanters rose up in rebellion. The uprising was quickly quashed when the Covenanter Army met with defeat at the Battle of Bothwell Bridge on June 22 of that year. Hundreds of rebel prisoners were marched to Edinburgh and given over to Mackenzie and installed in Greyfriars Kirkyard, an ironic move since that's where the movement had begun at a meeting in 1638. There, the rebels stayed in what amounted to little more than an animal pen, underfed and exposed to the elements. Hundreds died of exposure and disease during the winter, with only a few surviving. The leaders were beheaded, which was at least a quick death. Their heads adorned various public squares and main roads as a grisly reminder of what happened to those who had defied the king.

Mackenzie hunted down Covenanters wherever he could find them. Some historians estimate he killed 18,000 of them in what has become known as "the Killing Time." Others say this number is highly inflated, but he certainly earned the nickname of "Bloody Mackenzie."

When it came Mackenzie's turn to die in 1691, he was installed in a fine family mausoleum only a few yards from the former site of the prison, a distinctive, circular structure of grey stone, topped with a dome. The entrance room is empty, and a narrow flight of spiral stairs winds down to where the coffins of Mackenzie and three of his relatives lie.

It was after Bloody Mackenzie was laid to rest that the hauntings began there. At first, all was quiet at the mausoleum, but it is said that a highwayman named John Hayes fled there sometime in the 18th century. On the run from the law, he hid in a place he figured no one would look for him: inside Mackenzie's mausoleum. He is reputed to have lived there for six months, only coming out to steal the occasional food and drink. Eventually, someone spotted him returning "home" from one of his foraging expeditions and informed the authorities. When they stormed in to arrest him, they found Hayes had gone completely mad, raving that the coffins would move about at night and that Mackenzie could be heard scraping at the inside of the coffin as if trying to get out.

The mausoleum was resealed and remained quiet for a time. Then, in 1998, the mausoleum was broken into again, this time by a homeless man who had wanted to get out of the rain. He passed through the first room, opened a grate to the stairs leading to the lower room where the coffins of Mackenzie and his kinfolk were kept, and went down there. As he stepped onto the lower floor, the old wood gave way, and he crashed through and into a hitherto unknown third room, landing in a viscous, rotting mass of corpses in a plague pit from one of the many epidemics that had swept through Scotland. The people had been thrown into the pit together, probably in several cartloads of corpses gathered throughout the city, before the room was quickly sealed up, which probably accounts for the preservation of the corpses. Shrieking in terror and covered in rotting flesh, the homeless man scrambled out of the pit, having decided that a night in the rain didn't sound so bad after all. He shot up the stairs and straight across the churchyard, passing by a night watchman who had come to investigate the sounds. The sight of a screaming man covered in rotting flesh made the watchman scream as well, and he ran off into the night as fast as the homeless man.

Ever since the Mackenzie mausoleum and the plague vault were disturbed on that stormy night, people have reported strange phenomena around the place. Accounts started as soon as the next day, when a local woman walking past the mausoleum noticed it had been broken into and she peeked inside, only to be blown off her feet by a cold wind. Other passersby have seen strange shadows flitting in and out of the mausoleum. Loud noises emanate from it at night, such as the sound of a heavy, wooden object being dragged over stone.

When a woman was found unconscious nearby, her neck covered in bruises she later swore had been made by an invisible assailant that tried to strangle her, the city council put a new lock and gate on the structure and posted a no trespassing sign, but it did not stop the activity around the haunted vault. Police are regularly called in to deal with people claiming to have been slapped or pinched by unseen hands. Small animals are often found sacrificed at the entrance.

Even though the vault is off-limits to the general public unless they are with an accredited guide, it stands in the middle of a public cemetery, so countless people still witness strange goings-on. Many experience cold breezes coming from out of nowhere, or spots that are inexplicably much colder than the surrounding area. The attacks from the invisible entity often leave bruises and broken fingers behind. As recently as October 20, 2017, the *Edinburgh Evening News* reported that a man there had been scratched by an invisible attacker.

The poltergeist phenomena show no signs of abating. Ghost hunters theorize Bloody Mackenzie is not the only problem, instead blaming the more recently released ghosts from the plague pit. Indeed, the hauntings seem to have become much worse since the pit's discovery than at any previous time in the mausoleum's long history. The spirits were probably stirred up even more when two teenagers, no doubt encouraged by the place's reputation, broke into the mausoleum and stole a skull. Police found them playing football with it.

What's unusual about the Mackenzie Poltergeist is that it has endured for so long and is not attached to any one particular living person. Normally, poltergeists are associated with girls going through puberty, prompting some parapsychologists to theorize they are some sort of hormonal psychic projection. The girls seem to act as focal points, and unlike what might happen in a haunted house or castle, if the girls move to another location, the hauntings move with them. All that is well and good, but pubescent boys have just as many hormones raging through their systems as pubescent girls yet are rarely associated with poltergeist phenomena. The Mackenzie Poltergeist is a rare exception in that it is focused around a particular spot and not an individual, so while the entity manifests like a poltergeist, it has many aspects of a traditional ghost.

The hauntings in Greyfriars Kirkyard are not confined to Bloody Mackenzie's mausoleum. Indeed, they can be found all across the extensive burial ground.

Walking through the burial ground is a creepy experience. The monuments date from as early as 1561, when the cemetery was founded, to the middle of the 20th century, and they serve as an outdoor museum of strange funerary art in which grey stone skulls leer at visitors, angels weep over the dead, and the likenesses of the dead peer out, their faces frozen in time. One odd feature is the mortsafe, a thick iron cage built around the burial plot to keep the notorious resurrection men out. In the 18th century and early 19th century, it was illegal for surgeons to procure corpses for dissection unless they were that of a condemned criminal, for which dissection was a part of their sentence. Dissection was looked upon with such horror that only the worst criminals received it as their punishment. This meant that medical students were denied a vital part of their education, but where there is a demand, there is a supply. Enter the resurrection men, those who dug up bodies of the recently dead to offer them to medical schools at a price. Only the thick iron bars of the mortsafes could keep them at bay.

The Kirkyard appears to have been built on a hill, but that's not exactly true. Back in the 16th century, the place was a shallow depression, but so many people were buried there in the ensuing

400 years that the depression filled up, slowly rising up to form the hill found there today. No one knows how many souls are buried there, but estimates rise to half a million. Most are rather shallow graves, and those who visit after one of Edinburgh's frequent heavy rains might see the white gleam of a bone sticking out of the dark soil.

Visitors peeking through the iron fence at night or strolling through the Kirkyard in the broad daylight have seen white figures floating between the tombstones, and they have heard faint moans and children's laughter coming from nowhere. The worst hauntings—such as the attacks—are centered around the Mackenzie mausoleum, but paranormal phenomena can occur even at the opposite end of the extensive burial ground.

The old neighborhoods of central Edinburgh are a labyrinth of narrow streets and alleys called "closes." In the days before street lighting, all sorts of nefarious activities took place in their dark confines, so it is no wonder that many an old close is home to its own particular ghost. One of these is Brodie's Close, just off the Royal Mile, Edinburgh's main street, leading up to the famous castle. William "Deacon" Brodie was a well-respected town council member in the 18th century who worked as a cabinetmaker and locksmith. He was considered one of the most trustworthy men of his day, and no one hesitated to allow him to work on the front doors of their houses, which proved to be a mistake because he lived a double life as a thief. When he installed a new lock for someone, he always made a duplicate key. Then, he'd bide his time in order to allay any suspicions before sneaking into the home when he knew the residents were away and helping himself to whatever he liked. Brodie wouldn't have needed the money if he lived an honest life—his profession was a successful one—but he was an avid gambler and kept two mistresses with whom he had five children.

Brodie was eventually caught, as most thieves are, and hanged in 1788 in front of a huge crowd, said to have numbered 40,000. The 1791 census counted only 82,706 people in the entire city, so it was obviously a big day. This gawping crowd wasn't the last to see him, because now his ghost wanders up and down Brodie's Close at night, rattling a large ring of keys.

Many other landmarks in town are haunted, too. One of the most notorious is the Learmonth Hotel, a 19th century building with an abundance of poltergeist activity. Unlike ghosts who are seen, heard, and sometimes felt, poltergeists are unseen spirits who move objects. The word comes from the German *poltern* ("to make noise") and *Geist* ("ghost" or "spirit"), and that's exactly what the poltergeists at the Learmonth Hotel do. Doors open and shut by themselves, and sometimes the guests get locked out of their rooms so the spirits can play inside, turning on electrical appliances and whistling strange tunes. Staffers have become resigned to the paranormal goings-on and try to reassure the guests that poltergeists rarely actually hurt anyone.

Then there is Edinburgh's fabled underground warren of tunnels and rooms, called the Vaults. These are a series of corridors and connected, vaulted rooms that run under the city, and have been there for at least two hundred years, perhaps longer. Nobody is all that sure, but it appears that, as is the case with the Paris catacombs, they have been added to over the years. The main line of vaults are actually a series of 19 subterranean arches holding up the city's South Bridge, finished in 1788, but the subterranean passageways extend further than that. Some rooms have been sealed off and converted into pubs and underground nightclubs. Others sit empty.

Kjetil Bjørnsrud's pictures of parts of the Vaults

They were not always so. In the 18th and 19th centuries, there were a large number of indigent rural folk who came to Edinburgh, hoping to find a means of making a living, and ended up sleeping in the Vaults for lack of a better shelter. It was cold, it was damp, and it was pitch dark, but at least it was free.

It was also dangerous. Thieves, murderers, and body snatchers prowled the darkness, and many times the poor residents of the Vaults were awoken by pitiful screams of hapless victims. It is said that many of these victims still lurk in the Vaults today, tied to the place where they suffered in life. It is certainly a disconcerting place. The author visited the Vaults one night with a guide and found them cold and clammy, with strange sounds echoing off the stone walls. Since the Vaults run under inhabited buildings and busy roads, sounds get captured and rebound off the stone, intermingling in strange, eerie ways. It is easy to imagine such a place to be haunted.

One room has been converted into the worship center of a local coven of witches. These are not the witches of fable, but modern practitioners of Wicca, a recognized religion that attempts to recreate and preserve the old folk religion of Europe. Some of the 21st century witches had to cast many purification spells against hostile sprits to cleanse their worship area before they could practice their craft in peace, but the witches were only able to clean out their own vault. Others are still the lairs of angry spirits who appear faintly to living visitors, or whose footsteps still echo down the passageways.

Some of the ghosts are said to be the victims of William Burke and William Hare, the two most notorious resurrection men in Scottish history. In the early 19th century, the law made it extremely difficult for surgeons to procure corpses for dissection, so medical students were denied a vital part of their education. To compensate for this, resurrection men dug up the bodies of the recently dead and offered them to medical schools at a price.

Hare and Burke

Burke and Hare were two Irish immigrants who'd worked various jobs before hitting upon this grim mode of making a living. It is unknown how they ended up as friends, but at some point, Burke moved into Hare's home, where he let out spare rooms to lodgers, and the two made an unlikely partnership. Hare was described, by all contemporary accounts, as a drunken brawler, and a brute. Burke was more educated and professed to be a religious man, although he, too, drank to excess.

Both turned out to be cold-blooded killers. Their first crime came by a stroke of luck, as a contemporary broadside recounts: "In December 1827, a man died in Hare's house, whose body they sold to the Anatomists for £10. Getting so much money at a time when they were in a state of poverty, prompted them to look after means of the same kind, and the subject of murder was often talked over betwixt Hare and [Burke]. The first victim was an old woman belonging to Gilmerton, whom Hare had observed intoxicated on the street, and enticed into his house; they stupified her with more whisky, and put her to death in the way they pursued ever afterwards, by covering and pressing upon the nose and mouth with their hands. The body was carried to Surgeon's Square, and the money readily obtained for it."

The two men justified the sale of the body with the fact that the tenant had owed Hare £4. They had no justification for their second victim, another lodger, whom they got drunk and then suffocated.

In total they were charged with murdering 16 people, all of whom were sold to Dr. Robert Knox, a surgeon who used to lecture on human anatomy by dissecting corpses in front of a paying audience. The bodies were delivered in a large tea chest, the two men acting like they were workers with a delivery for the Surgeons' Hall. Many of the victims were lured into Hare's boarding house, given plenty of liquor, and then strangled. One of the victims was a mentally disabled teenage boy.

The two resurrection men also did away with an old woman and her 12 year-old mute grandson. While Hare smothered the old woman, Burke bent the child over his knee and broke his back. Later, while awaiting execution in prison, Burke confessed that this killing troubled him the most of all his crimes, and that he couldn't get the boy's dying expression out of his head. The tea chest they usually used to deliver the victims proved to be too small to fit both bodies, so they used a herring barrel instead. The two resurrection men put it on a cart drawn by Hare's horse, but when the animal wouldn't pull the heavy load up the steep hill to the Surgeons' Hall, they had to hire a third man—who was unaware of the barrel's grisly contents—to help them move it. Once Hare returned home, he was so infuriated with his horse that he shot it.

Burke and Hare generally had to get drunk to get up the courage to commit their crimes. At his trial, Burke confessed that he "could not sleep at night without a bottle of whisky by his bedside, and a twopenny candle to burn all night beside him; when he awoke he would take a draught of the bottle—sometimes half a bottle at a draught—and that would make him sleep." Clearly, his troubled conscience didn't stop him from committing more murders.

That such a series of killings, all in the space of a single year, should go undetected is testament to the misery in which Edinburgh's poor had to live. The victims were mostly indigent, or poor and working jobs such as junk collectors, and the authorities simply didn't care about them. The killings were almost exposed when the body of the mentally disabled young man was delivered to Dr. Knox. Several of the students recognized him because he was a common and well-known figure who'd wandered the streets, but Knox denied it was him and quickly began the dissection, soon making the corpse unrecognizable. The students made no more fuss about the matter.

Dr. Knox

As Sir Walter Scott would later quip, "Our Irish importation have made a great discovery of Oeconomicks, namely, that a wretch who is not worth a farthing while alive, becomes a valuable article when knockd on the head & carried to an anatomist; and acting on this principle, have cleard the streets of some of those miserable offcasts of society, whom nobody missed because nobody wishd to see them again."

The pair only got caught because a pair of Hare's lodgers, who had somehow survived up to this point, stumbled upon one of the murder victims before Burke and Hare could move the body. By the time the police arrived, they had delivered the body to Knox, but they soon broke down under questioning. It wasn't long before both of them were up before a judge.

The court was faced with a problem, however. They did not have firm evidence for any of the killings except the last, and there was no evidence the final victim had died by violence. The court decided to offer Hare to turn King's evidence, making him free from prosecution if he fingered Burke. This he did, and Burke was found guilty, sentenced to hang, and then have his body publicly dissected.

As one broadside dating to 1829 covering the hanging of William Burke gleefully reported, "His struggles were long and violent, and his body was agonizingly convulsed. We observed that his fall was unusually short, scarcely more than three inches, the noose instead of being as is usual, immediately behind his ear, was at the very summit of the vertebrae. We should have mentioned that when the rope was placed about his neck there was a universal cry raised of 'Burke him;' and, during the whole of the horrible process, there were repeated crys of Hare, Hare. A precentor or clerk was upon the scaffold, as it had been arranged that he should exercise his function; but such were the indications of the feelings of the populace, that those in authority saw it prudent to dispense with this part of the ceremony. Great attempts were made by the Magistrates, officers and others in attendance, upon the scaffold, by signals, to silence the mob during the putting up of prayers; but their efforts were altogether ineffectual. At every struggle the wretch made when suspended, a most rapturous shout was raised by the multitude. When the body was cut down, at three quarters past eight, the most frightful yell we ever heard was raised by the indignant populace, who manifested the most eager desire to get the monster's carcase within their clutches, to gratify their revenge, even after the law had been satisfied, by tearing it to pieces. They were only restrained by the bold front presented by the police. We observed the persons under the scaffold, with knives and scissors, possessing themselves of part of the rope and even slipping into their pockets some of the shavings from the coffin. The scramble at this time was of the most extraordinary nature ever witnessed at an execution in this country."

An illustration of Burke's execution

The surgeon who performed the dissection was Professor Alexander Monro, who, ironically enough, was the man Burke and Hare had originally intended to sell their first victim to. By chance, Munro wasn't around when they delivered the body, and so they ended up selling it to Knox. During the dissection, which attracted record crowds, Monro dipped a quill pen into the dead man's blood and wrote "This is written with the blood of Wm Burke, who was hanged at Edinburgh. This blood was taken from his head."

Burke's skull was given to the Edinburgh Phrenological Society for study. Phrenology is a quack medical belief that was popular at that time. It proposed the theory that a person's character and intellect could be perceived by studying the bumps on his head. Burke must have had some fascinating bumps. The residents of Edinburgh were fascinated by his skin too, and they cut it up, tanned it into leather, and used it to make wallets.

Modern visitors can still see relics from this horrible chapter in Edinburgh's history. Burke's skeleton is on display at the Anatomical Museum of the Edinburgh Medical School. The phrenologists eventually tired of fondling the murderer's skull and reunited it with the skeleton for the sake of posterity. Over at the museum housed in Old Surgeons' Hall, yoneou can see his death mask, and a book supposedly bound in his tanned skin. Some of Knox's surgical instruments are also on display. While the Burke skin wallets have all disappeared, a calling card case made from the skin of the back of his left hand is on display at the Cadies & Witchery Tours museum.

Kim Traynor's picture of Old Surgeons' Hall

Despite Burke's inglorious end, his victims have not been able to rest. Locals whisper that some of the screams that can be heard echoing through the Vaults at night are those of the poor people the two men murdered. Others hear the rumble of the resurrection men's cart in the street outside the Old Surgeons' Hall. Perhaps the spirits are restless because Hare got off "Scot-free," and Knox also escaped prosecution because Burke insisted throughout the trial that the surgeon did not know the bodies were those of murder victims. Even the passage of the Anatomy Act of 1832, which made it easier to obtain cadavers for dissection, and which was a direct result of the Burke and Hare murders, did not lay the spirits to rest. To this day they call for justice from beyond the grave.

Haunted Pubs and Churches

Parapsychologists say that ghosts are often tied to places that were important to them in life. Someone who suffered a violent death may linger in the spot where he met his end, while others may continue to pass down a road they frequented while they were still among the living. Thus, it is not surprising that many ghosts haunt two places important to most Scots: the church and the pub. Both are places where people seek solace, and both are often old buildings that have seen their share of history.

Some of them even keep their dead residents after falling into ruin. One such building is St. Andrew's Cathedral, founded in the 12th century. As is the case with many of Europe's great cathedrals, it took generations to build and was dedicated in 1318 in a ceremony attended by Robert the Bruce. Soon, pilgrims from all over the land were coming to St. Andrew's to hear the sermons and pray for miracles from Scotland's patron saint. Several relics from St. Andrew himself were housed in the cathedral, including one of his teeth, an arm bone, a kneecap, and three fingers. The magnificent 12th century building was actually built atop a much older church that may date all the way back to 700, well before the land was completely Christianized, and St. Andrew's relics had their home there before receiving a much grander building. The relics drew pilgrims to the site at a time when many believed in their miraculous healing powers.

Like so many fine houses of worship, it fell prey to the Scottish Reformation, during which the country broke with the Catholic Church. In the process, it was stripped of its ornaments in 1559 and abandoned in 1561.

After almost 500 years of neglect, much of the cathedral has vanished, but what remains is stunning in its grandeur. Parts of the wall survive with their original arches, as does the east gable of the presbytery that once housed St. Andrew's relics. These impressive twin towers and connecting arches somehow survived while much of the rest of the building was dismantled and the stones reused for later buildings.

The tallest part of the cathedral is St. Rule's tower, the last remnant of the cathedral's predecessor, St. Rule's Church, built around 1130. The square tower is 33 meters (108 feet) high. The views from the top of it are truly magnificent, with the ruins of the cathedral, the nearby town, and sea all laid out beneath.

Robert de Montrose, a prior of St. Andrews from 1387-1394, enjoyed the view so much, he went up almost every night to get a glimpse, especially when the moon was full. By all accounts, Robert de Montrose was a kindly and fair man, but in his office as prior, he sometimes had to be the disciplinarian. Once, the case of a monk who had committed a number of crimes, including fornication, came before him, and Robert was forced to punish the man severely. The monk took his punishment, but resentment grew within him. One fine, moonlit night, when the goodly prior climbed to the top of the tower, the monk quietly followed him. The prior was too entranced by the view to either see or hear him, and the monk drew a dagger from his pocket, stabbed the prior in the back, and pushed him out the window to fall to his death.

Nevertheless, the prior still sometimes makes the climb to the top of the tower, especially on those clear, moonlit nights he so loved. Visitors have seen him standing at the window, a beatific smile on his lips, while less fortunate witnesses have seen him falling to the ground. Of course, they rush to the spot to help, but they never find a body.

Despite his cruel end, Robert de Montrose has remained just as kindly as ever. An account from 1948 tells how a visitor was climbing the tower when he came to a dark area, unlit by the tower's then-meager lighting. His foot slipped on a worn step, and he had to grab onto the handrail to keep from tumbling down the stone steps and probably getting killed. Just then, he noticed a man wearing a cassock standing on the stairs above him. The clergyman addressed him in a low, pleasant voice, telling him it was all right and that the visitor could hold onto him for safety. The man replied that he was all right now and moved past the figure. Only when he got to the top did he realize he hadn't felt anything when he brushed by the man in the cassock. When he had made it back down and asked the watchman, he learned that no one had been up there but him, and that he must have met old Robert de Montrose.

Another, less personable ghost also supposedly inhabits these ruins. Enclosing the cathedral precinct is a protective wall that once had 16 towers, although a few have now disappeared. One of the survivors is a two-story structure positioned just east of the cathedral's east gable. It is there that nighttime visitors sometimes see the White Lady. She is seen in many places on the property, but when she appears, she is always heading toward the tower, vanishing once she gets there. People describe her as a beautiful woman floating over the ground in a flowing white dress and wearing white leather gloves. She has been seen for at least 200 years, although no one knows who she is.

In 1868, two masons repairing the tower discovered a hidden room containing several coffins, and all of them were closed except for one containing the well-preserved remains of a woman wearing a white dress and white gloves. There were no clues as to why that particular coffin was open. Some theorize that the dead woman had been robbed of her jewelry, while others claim the ghost herself opened it. The coffins were all reburied, but that hasn't stopped the White Lady from appearing now and then, near where her eternal rest had once been disturbed.

Another old house of worship with resident ghosts is Culross Abbey, founded in 1217 on the hallowed spot where Saint Serf built a church in the 6th century to convert pagans. Much of it is now a picturesque ruin, although the eastern section still functions as the parish church. Local legend says there's a secret tunnel running from the abbey for an unknown distance beneath the countryside. Somewhere down there, a spirit sits on a golden chair, waiting to give an immense treasure to whoever finds him.

A blind piper once decided to go in search of the spirit and descended into the tunnel with his dog. He played his pipes to signal his progress to those above, and a curious crowd followed him for nearly a mile before the piping suddenly stopped. Several days later, the dog reappeared, but the piper never returned. Within the abbey grounds, many have seen processions of ghostly monks filing past, intent on their prayers even after they had gone to achieve their eternal reward.

Kim Traynor's picture of the abbey

Many of Scotland's old pubs and wayside inns are haunted as well. One of the most famous is the Drovers Inn in the town of Inverarnan, along the River Falloch, near the head of Loch Lomond. The town and inn have long been a stopping point for travelers looking for a meal, a few pints, and a bed. In the early days, before the old coaching routed, Highland drovers led their herds to the Lowlands for sale. In later years, steamboats passed up and down the loch. Nowadays, it's a popular rest stop for hikers along the West Highland Way, one of Scotland's great trails.

The region acted as a boundary in ancient times. A stone circle stands near the village, and many archaeologists theorize that these circles marked meeting places for different tribes. Nearby stands the Stone of the Britons, a natural outcropping that served as a boundary stone for three kingdoms: Pictland to the east; Dumbarton and Strathclyde to the south; and Dál Riata to the northwest. Thus, it was the meeting point for the Picts, the Britons, and the Scots.

The area has been a focal point for centuries, and such places often act as a magnet for the paranormal. Several spots in the town of Inverarnan and the surrounding countryside are said to be haunted, but most haunted of all is the Drovers Inn, founded in 1705 and named for the many drovers who have found rest and relaxation there over the years.

The oldest ghost to inhabit the inn dates to 1792. Locally known as the "Year of the Sheep," it was the same year many landlords decided that raising sheep was more profitable than parceling out the land to tenant farmers, so they evicted hundreds of families. These people, already poor, lost their sole means of income and were left to fend for themselves in the middle of winter.

One family, a young couple with a little boy, lived a couple of days' walk from the Drovers Inn. They decided to head south to find work, perhaps to the Lowlands or to one of England's cities get a job in one of the new factories. They trudged their weary way down the old drovers' road through the first day and slept in the open that night. On the second day, half-dead from the cold, they knew they had to make it to the Drovers Inn to find shelter or they would surely perish. When a storm blew in, the family became disoriented, never made it to the inn, and froze to death like so many other families that dreadful winter. Now, on cold winter evenings, hikers arriving late at the Drovers Inn sometimes tell of having seem a bedraggled family in old-style clothing struggling through the snow and wind. The family is also seen inside the inn itself. A couple staying in Room Two awoke in the middle of the night, freezing cold. At first, they thought the heating had broken, but then, at the foot of the bed, they saw the sad, little family, shivering in the icy air. The boy waved to them forlornly, and then the sad scene vanished.

Another chilling experience sometimes happens in Room Six. Someone will be sleeping soundly when they suddenly awaken, cold and wet. They open their eyes and are shocked to see a small girl lying next to them, soaking wet and radiating a bone-chilling cold. When the girl vanishes, the room slowly returns to its normal temperature. The startled guest, however, generally doesn't get any more sleep.

The girl is the phantom of a real child who drowned in the River Falloch, just behind the inn. She was playing with her doll after a hard rain in the early part of the century. The river ran high and fast, and the unsupervised child strayed too close to it. She dropped her doll into the water by accident, and when she tried to retrieve it, she was swept away and drowned. Some local men found her, brought back her to the inn, and put her in Room Six until they could summon the authorities. The doll was never recovered, though it is sometimes seen, walking around like a miniature person, searching for the lost little girl who had once loved it so much.

Other ghosts haunt the inn as well, such as the shade of a cattle drover who was murdered by thieves. There are also strange light orbs that flit around the rooms at night. A stay in this inn can definitely come with a bonus experience.

In the town of Kirkcaldy, Fife, about halfway between St. Andrew's and Edinburgh, there are at least two haunted pubs. The Feuars Arms, a well-preserved Victorian pub, is a center of poltergeist activity. People have felt an invisible hand tap them on their shoulders or heard footsteps running up and down the stairs when there is no one there. The beer pumps sometimes turn themselves on or off as well, and the staff report the cellar is unusually cold and forbidding. Back in 2005, a team of paranormal investigators examined the pub, and several witnesses saw a glass slide across a table when no one was touching it.

Betty Nicols, a pub which first appeared in town records in 1741 but is probably older, has been serving drinks for generations. It is now a gastropub, and it has also seen a number of strange events over the years. Once, a cleaning lady came in the early morning to find the pub locked up and deserted, but she found a candle burning at one of the tables. It must have been lit in the wee hours of the morning because it was a small tea light, the kind that only burns for a couple of hours. Curious as to who had created this obvious fire hazard, the owners of the pub reviewed CCTV footage, and, to their astonishment, they saw the candle light up on its own. No one was seen on the tape between closing time and when the cleaner arrived the next morning.

While most ghostly encounters happen late at night when all is quiet, visitors to this pub often experience hauntings when the place is full. The shadowy figures of two men and a dog are sometimes seen crossing the bar. Pay close attention when looking into the mirrors, and some of the people seen in the mirrors might not actually be standing in the room.

Like the Feuars Arms, the cellar in Betty Nicols is cold and disturbing. Many of the staff have complained that they feel as if they are being watched when they do.

Remote Ghosts

Some of the greatest attractions in Scotland are its many wild and remote areas. Millions of visitors enjoy wonderful days hiking across its rugged landscape without seeing another person. Of course, that isn't to say there aren't any souls about; in fact, Scotland's more isolated areas seem to attract ghosts.

Take Cape Wrath, for instance. This rugged spit of land on the extreme northwest coast is one of the most dramatic spots in Scotland, and one of its most remote. The area is made up of jagged sea cliffs and bleak moorland, much of it owned by the Ministry of Defense, so few people go there. The nearest village is ten miles away. There is also a lighthouse at the cape, which is where the ghost resides.

Built in 1828, the lighthouse run automatically since 1998, but a lighthouse keeper manned it before then. During that period, the lighthouse received regular visitors, some who came to supply the keeper as well as some adventuresome hikers wanting to see one of Scotland's most dramatic and remote locations. Many have reported a strange apparition near the ruined cottage not far from the lighthouse. He appears as a tall man, well over 6' tall, wearing a three-cornered hat, knee-length boots, and a long, dark coat. He is seen quite clearly and looks real, unlike the transparent or glowing apparitions witnessed in other locations, but he will vanish if anyone approaches. Local lore says he was the captain of a ship that smashed on the rocks in the 18th century before the lighthouse had been installed. Now, he wanders the spot where he and his crew drowned, keeping an eye on the shipping and making sure the lighthouse remains lit. Some ghost hunters have joked the place would be better called "Cape Wraith." Sightings of the captain have waned in recent years, perhaps because fewer people visit the spot or perhaps because the spirit is simply fading away as spirits sometimes do.

Scotland is fringed with islands, windswept by harsh North Atlantic and North Sea winds and rains that have bred tough, independent people and many local traditions. The Orkney Islands, 10 miles (16 kilometers) off the north coast of Scotland, are the most hospitable, with a relatively mild if wet climate and a population of more than 20,000 on its approximately 70 islands. There is a great deal of debate in local pubs as to what constitutes an island, as opposed to nothing more than a rock sticking out from the sea. These rocks are often called skerries, but the dividing line between skerry and island is not altogether clear. A general definition for a skerry is that it is too small to be inhabited, but even that doesn't settle the debate. For example, there's a rock in the harbor of Kirkwall, the islands' capital, about the size of a large living room. It has a bit of grass on it and not much else. Could this be classified as a skerry? Some may say so, as the rock was inhabited at times, used as a prison for unfortunate Norsemen who were marooned there in plain view of the mainland. Needless to say, they didn't survive long.

This rock does not appear to harbor any ghosts, but many spots in the Orkney Islands do. Many of them are those of young children, unfortunate enough to have died before being baptized. This was a frequent occurrence in the more remote islands because of the lack of priests. Some children waited years before being baptized as a result.

Two children on the island of North Ronaldsay suffered such a fate. At some time in the early 19th century, they both died from an illness and were buried in the garden by their bereaved parents. Thus, not only did they die unbaptized, they were denied a Christian burial. The garden stood by a lane, and passersby often report a feeling of dread coming from the place. At dusk, strange, white birds fly straight up into the sky. At night, eerie lights bob around the enclosure. Things got so bad that the locals investigated, found the remains of the two children, and gave them a proper burial in the island's little churchyard. Though no one feels a sense of uncanny fear while passing the churchyard these days, nor do they see white birds, the strange lights still make an occasional appearance. Perhaps they are the spirits of the children, wondering where their home had gone.

Clearly, a Christian burial is no guarantee of a peaceful spirit if the dead are disturbed. Such was the case of Baubie Skithawa on the island of Sanday.

Baubie Skithawa was an old woman who had led what passed for a prosperous life on the islands. She had a good farmstead, plenty to eat, and clothes on her back. When she was dying, she made her final purchase: a set of new clothes and a winding-sheet of fine material she found at the Lammas Fair in Kirkwall, the capital of Orkney. Old Baubie had always taken good care of her appearance, and she wanted to look good in the afterlife, too.

When the time came for her to pass on, the local midwife laid her out for her wake, dressed her in her final outfit, and wrapped her in her fine winding-sheet. All her neighbors came by to pay their respects, including one strange old recluse everyone called "Black Jock" because her ancestors supposedly made a deal with the Devil to cast black magic. Since everyone feared her, no one dared object to her presence. As everyone sat the night through with the body, a custom that is now rarely honored, she was heard several times to have muttered what a pity it was that such nice clothing and such a nice winding-sheet should be buried.

After the proper observances, Baubie Skithawa was buried in the graveyard at Cross Kirk. A couple of days later, Black Jock snuck into the cemetery, dug the body up, stripped it naked, and stole the clothing and winding-sheet for herself. She took these items home and hid them.

Black Jock covered her tracks well. She had been getting up to all sorts of mischief throughout her life, and she knew how to hide her crimes. Black Jock placed the sod back onto the grave so expertly that the gravedigger himself wouldn't have noticed that the plot had been disturbed, but the dead have their own ways of warning the living. The day after poor old Baubie's grave was desecrated, a young man named Andrew Moodie walked past the graveyard at dusk and saw the most frightening sight of his life. The sky turned suddenly black, the clouds roiled, and lightning flashed. Pillars of fire shot from the churchyard, rising high into the sky. At the top of each pillar hovered the spirits of the dead, waving their arms, their grave clothes and winding-sheets fluttering in the hard wind, beckoning to each other as if to attract the other's attention. They gestured to one pillar, in particular, seeming to laugh and mock the spirit floating atop it. Andrew Moodie quickly saw why - it was the spirit of Baubie Skithawa, stark naked in the fiery night, wailing with shame and anger as she tried to cover her nakedness.

Needless to say, Andrew Moodie fled from that place as fast as his feet would carry him to the nearest cottage, which happened to be that of Black Jock. There, he pounded on the door, begging to be let in. At first, Black Jock refused him entry, but he put up such a racket that she finally relented. Young Andrew shot into the cottage as soon as the door opened. Black Jock slammed it shut behind him, barring it with a wooden yoke into which she stuck three iron awls. Iron, of course, is a sure charm against spirits. Andrew felt a bit safer upon seeing this, although, like everyone else on Sanday, he steered clear of Black Jock under normal circumstances.

The storm still raged outside, and Black Jock raged at her unwelcome guest. She told him to sit in a corner and keep his mouth shut. Then, as the thunder banged and the lightning flashed, Black Jock took pieces of sod and stuffed every hole in the house—the window, the smoke hole, even the cat hole above the door, an old feature of traditional Orcadian architecture. Then she sat in the center of the room, picked up a needle, and drew circles around herself on the dirt floor.

Outside, the storm grew in intensity, and Andrew heard another sound besides the wind, thunder, and lightning. It sounded like the cries of a host of people, wailing and speaking all at once. One by one, the pieces of sod that stopped up the holes in the house were pushed out, and ghostly hands reached inside. Andrew cowered in the corner of the room as Black Jock continued her incantations, her face a mask of terror.

Then Baubie Skithawa's pale face appeared at the window. "Give me back my grave clothes!" she cried. "Give me back my winding-sheet! I am cold! I am colder than death! Oh, what a torture it is to be shameful and naked in the cold, wet earth. Give them back to me!" A ghostly arm reached through the cat hole and down to the bolt barring the door. The phantom hand touched one of the iron awls that had been driven into the bolt and recoiled, for no spirit can touch iron. The ghosts wailed in frustration. Andrew realized that it was near dawn and the ghosts would soon have to return from whence they came.

The spirit of Baubie Skithawa screamed at the window and then stretched forth, elongating unnaturally and reaching its head and arms into the room. The ghostly hands tried to grab Black Jock but were repelled by the magic circle the witch had drawn around herself. Then they reached for Andrew where he was cowering in the corner and slapped him on the top of the head. The force of the blow knocked him down, and as he fell, his foot scraped over the circle in the dirt floor, breaking the magic and knocking the needle out of Black Jock's hand. The witch knew the game was up, and she raced to her chest by the foot of her bed, flung it open, and pulled out the stolen winding-sheet and grave clothing. As soon as she did, they flew out of her hands and straight out the window. With a cry of victory, the spirits withdrew. Then, an invisible force smacked into Black Jock and laid her flat on the floor.

To his profound relief, Andrew heard the cockcrow. The storm abated, no more wails came from without, and all grew calm. But all was not well. His head stung from the blow he had received, and when he reached up to rub it, he discovered a bald spot in the shape of a palm and five fingers. No hair would ever grow there again.

Black Jock was worse off. She lay where she had been knocked down, and when Andrew tried to pull her up, he found no amount of force would budge her. The young man ran for help, telling all the neighbors of the terrible things he had witnessed. They, too, tried to pull Black Jock up, but with no success, so they summoned Mansie Peace, a local cunning man who had a great amount of experience in such matters. He walked around her prone body seven times, chanting seven prayers. Then, he boiled seven bluestones in water, allowed the water to cool, and poured the water over Black Jock. She was finally able to rise, and when she got to her feet, she was a changed woman. Never again did she pester her neighbors with magic, and never again did the graveyard at Cross Kirk have a ghostly apparition. Andrew Moodie, however, bore the mark of the ghostly hand on his scalp for the rest of his days.

The Shetland Islands are even more remote than Orkney. This archipelago of some 300 islands and skerries can be found 50 miles (80 kilometers) to the northeast of Orkney, blasted by Atlantic and North Sea storms. The islands are ringed with jagged cliffs and made up of low, rolling hills. Few trees grow there, and its industry is limited mostly to sheepherding, a bit of crofting, and fishing. There are also extensive oil and natural gas fields in the surrounding waters. The winters are harsh, and the summers short, but the Shetlanders love their islands and are proud of their traditions, but they're probably a little less proud having one of the most haunted houses in Britain.

Windhouse is the ruined home of a laird ("lord") that dates to the early 18th century. It sits on a hill by the settlement of Mid Yell, on the island of Yell, the second largest island in the archipelago besides Mainland. The Windhouse hasn't been inhabited since the 1930s and is now an empty ruin with little more than its walls still standing. True to its name, the hard sea wind howls through the empty corridors and glassless windows, creating an eerie feeling.

Even when it was in use, it was haunted. Residents complained of several different spirits waking them up from their sleep and flitting through the hallways. One such tale associated with the place is called "The Trow of Windhouse" and dates to the early 19th century. A "trow" is the local word for fairy folk, who come in various forms, as this tale shows.

One day, a sailor was shipwrecked on the shore nearby Yell, and he was the only survivor of the wreck. Having sunk in such a remote spot, no one came to help him. He managed to wade ashore, carrying a steel ax. He didn't know how or why he had grabbed it from the wreck, especially since it certainly hadn't helped him swim, but he had the feeling he might need it. The soaked sailor wandered around the bleak hills for a time until he saw Windhouse. He hurried to knock on the door to beg for help, and the laird and his family were kind enough to bring him in and let him warm by the fire. They also gave him some tea and food. The family was busy packing, however, and told the sailor that if he knew what was good for him, he'd leave with them. It was Christmas Eve, the family told him, and that date was always one of woe for the family, for every year a trow would visit them and carry one of them off.

The sailor was tired after his ordeal and didn't fear anything of this world or the next, so he opted to stay. The family shrugged their shoulders and cleared out. That night, the sailor discovered the family had spoken the truth when a huge, shapeless mass came up to the house. The hardy sailor showed no fear, and it only took one swipe of his trusty ax to fell the beast. The next morning was Christmas Day, the family returned, and the sailor told his tale. When he took them out to show where he had killed the trow, the body had disappeared. All that remained was a patch of heather—colored a bright green—that had grown higher than the surrounding plants. Locals still point out this patch of heather as proof of the story.

Locals say the dark forces associated with the site came from the fact the Windhouse had been built on a graveyard. There were gravestones found during construction, and the cemetery wasn't marked on any map, but everyone on the island firmly believed this to be true.

The ghosts haven't left. To this day, some visitors have spotted an elegant woman dressed in silk, supposedly the mistress of the house from a long-ago generation who met her end when she fell down the stairs and broke her neck. It is claimed that her skeleton was found beneath the main staircase at a later time. Why she was buried there rather than in the graveyard is unclear. Others say she was murdered.

A different staircase attracts the more humble ghost of a servant girl who walks up the steps even though the stairs themselves have long since rotted away. There's even the spirit of a dog who approaches brave hikers who venture to the spot. It seems friendly enough, but when the visitors try to pet it, the dog vanishes into thin air. Other manifestations include strange noises, shadows through which no light penetrates, dark figures who walk through walls, and feelings of dread in certain rooms. One bedroom produced such a feeling of fear in all who entered that no one would sleep there. A maid who worked at the house for many years refused to even make the bed because every time she attempted to do so, a booming laugh resonated throughout the room.

Residents have also reported cold breezes coming from nowhere, even when the windows were closed, and some rooms suddenly becoming ice cold. This is a common occurrence in haunted places. Ghost hunters theorize that when spirits try to manifest, they draw ambient energy from the surrounding air, causing the temperature to plummet.

On one occasion in the early 20th century, the family that lived there went for a walk and didn't return until after sunset. As they approached the dark house, the windows lit up one after the other until the entire house was ablaze with light, despite the fact the house had no electricity at the time. As the family stood there in utter shock, the lights went out one by one, as mysteriously as they had appeared.

Remarkably, in 2017, archaeologists discovered two skeletons on the site, confirming the long-held belief that Windhouse stood on a burial ground. Judging from artifacts found with the mortal remains, the cemetery dated to the 13th or 14th century, long before the house had been built. The graves were shallow, with only six inches of soil above them, no doubt because the soil layer in many areas of the rocky island is quite thin.

The excavations were done in preparation for the restoration of the house, which still continues. The team is convinced they will find more burials in the future. Perhaps their discoveries will help to finally lay the old spirits to rest.

The west coast of Scotland is fringed with hundreds of rocky islands, some small skerries, others major pieces of land. The largest island group is the Outer Hebrides, also known as the Western Isles, off the northwest coast. 15 of these islands are inhabited, while more than 50 others are not. Even the shortest visit to one of them will explain why, as the rugged, rocky hills are hard to build on and don't offer much soil for farming or grazing. They do, however, offer some of the most breathtaking scenery in all of the British Isles, so hardy travelers have their efforts richly rewarded.

One of the most popular destinations is also one of the kindest: the Isle Of Lewis. This is a misnomer since it's actually the northern part of the Isle of Lewis and Harris. Lewis is the flatter part, with the largest concentration of population in all the Outer Hebrides, as well as its biggest settlement, Stornoway. Stornoway has a population of more than 8,000, while Harris is mountainous and sparsely populated. They are so different that they might as well be different islands, and they are often referred to as such. The islanders' traditional lifestyle, arts and crafts, and the area's natural beauty attract a steady trickle of visitors.

One place they do not generally go except to zip along the road from Stornoway to Harris is Arnish Moor, a bleak, open wetland. It was on these moors more than three centuries ago that tragedy struck. Back around the year 1700, two boys decided to skip school and go out on Arnish Moor to collect grouse eggs, which make for a very tasty breakfast. After a few hours, they decided to go home, but they argued over who should get which number of eggs. One boy said he had collected more, while the other vehemently disagreed. The first boy got so incensed that he picked up a large stone and smacked his friend over the head with it. He probably meant only to hurt his friend, but the boy didn't know his own strength and caved the other boy's skull in. Panicked, the young murderer hid the body, ran off to the nearest port, and jumped on a ship to become a sailor.

The boy spent several years at sea, but he was an islander, born and bred, and he longed to see his home again. Eventually, he returned, having grown and changed so much that no one recognized him. He checked into a local inn at the edge of the moor and asked for supper. The landlady served his meal, giving him cutlery with unusual bone handles. When he commented on them, she replied that she had found a collection of sheep's bones buried out on the moor. The sailor's eyes grew wide. Had they truly been sheep's bones, or were they something more sinister? Not wanting to draw suspicion to himself, he tried to act casual and picked up the cutlery, even though he had lost his appetite.

While he tried to eat his meal, he felt something wet on his hands. When he looked down, he saw the bone handles of his knife and fork were oozing blood. There's an old Scottish saying that a murdered body will bleed if the murderer touches it, and in this case, it turned out to be true. The sailor went almost mad with fright and immediately confessed his old crime. The judge ordered him to be hanged.

Sadly, the murdered boy was never laid to rest. The landlady couldn't remember the exact spot where she had found the bones and thus couldn't give the complete skeleton a Christian burial, except for the grisly cutlery. Now, the boy wanders the moor, occasionally chasing motorists on the lonely stretch of road near where he was murdered. One motorcyclist swore he was speeding down the road and was chased by the shade of the boy for several miles.

In 1964, a much-decayed body was found half-buried on the moor, dressed in clothing typical of the late 17th century. When archaeologists examined the young male, they found he had died from a blow to the back of the head with a blunt, hard object. Was this the body of the young collector of grouse eggs uncovered at last? The body was identified as that of a man, aged between 20 and 25, which is too old to fit the story, and there were no missing bones.

Perhaps there are more bodies on the moor waiting to be found.

Online Resources

Other ghost titles by Charles River Editors & Sean McLachlan

Other titles about Scotland on Amazon

Bibliography

Bennett, H. "A murder victim discovered: clothing and other finds from an early 18th century grave on Arnish Moor, Lewis", *Proceedings of the Society of Antiquaries Scotland*, vol. 106, 1974-5. Pages 172-82.

Coleman, Loren and Jerome Clark. *Cryptozoology A To Z: The Encyclopedia of Loch Monsters, Sasquatch, Chupacabras, and Other Authentic Mysteries of Nature.* New York City, NY: Fireside Books, 1999.

Corliss, William R. *The Unexplained: A Sourcebook of Strange Phenomena.* New York City, NY: Bantam Books Inc., 1976.

Cornell, James. *The Monster of Loch Ness.* New York City, NY: Scholastic Book Services, 1977.

Coventry, Martin. *The Castles of Scotland: A Comprehensive Guide to More Than 4100 Castles, Towers, Historic Houses, Stately Homes and Family Lands* (5th Edition). Musselburgh, Scotland, United Kingdom: Goblinshead, 2001.

Forde, M.B. *Eerie Britain: Ten of Britain's Most Terrifying and Peculiar Real-Life Stories.* Kindle Direct Publishing, 2011.

Fort, Charles. *The Complete Books of Charles Fort.* New York City, NY: Dover Publications, 2003.

Green, Andrew. *Our Haunted Kingdom: more than 350 authenticated hauntings or case histories recorded in the UK over the past 25 years.* London, United Kingdom: Wolfe Publishing Ltd, 1973.

Ingram, John. *The Haunted Homes and Family Traditions of Great Britain.* London: Gibbings & Company, Ltd., 1897.

Jones, Richard Glyn. *Haunted Castles of Britain and Ireland.* New York City, NY: Barnes & Noble Books, 2003.

MacDonald, Hugh. *Rambles Around Glasgow.* London, United Kingdom: Thomas Murray, 1856.

Marwick, Ernest W. *The Folklore of Orkney and Shetland.* London, UK: BT Batsford Ltd., 1986.

McCloskey, Keith. *The Lighthouse: The Mystery of the Eilean Mor Lighthouse Keepers.* Stroud, Gloucestershire, UK: The History Press, 2014.

McLachlan, Sean. *Weird Scotland: Monsters, Mysteries, and Magic Across the Scottish Nation.* Charles River Editors, 2016.

Seafield, Lily. *Scottish Ghosts.* David Dale House, Scotland: Waverley Books Ltd, 2009.

Stewart, Gregor. *Ghosts of Scotland.* Greenock, Scotland, United Kingdom: Beul Aithris Publishing, 2017.

Underwood, Peter. *Where the Ghosts Walk: The Gazetteer of Haunted Britain.* London, UK: Souvenir Press, 2013.

Free Books by Charles River Editors

We have brand new titles available for free most days of the week. To see which of our titles are currently free, click on this link.

Discounted Books by Charles River Editors

We have titles at a discount price of just 99 cents everyday. To see which of our titles are currently 99 cents, click on this link.

Printed in Great Britain
by Amazon